Original title:
When Dreams Take Flight

Copyright © 2024 Creative Arts Management OÜ
All rights reserved.

Author: Gabriel Kingsley
ISBN HARDBACK: 978-9916-90-514-2
ISBN PAPERBACK: 978-9916-90-515-9

Spirals of Endless Potential

In the dance of stars we weave,
Dreams spin out, a web we believe.
Each thought a seed, in soil divine,
Sprouting hope, where futures align.

Winding paths through cosmic streams,
We chase the light of shining dreams.
With every turn, new visions rise,
Infinite realms beneath wide skies.

The Weightlessness of Wonder

Floating soft on morning's breeze,
Curiosity flows with ease.
The world unfolds in vibrant hues,
Each whisper brings a spark of news.

In moments small, great tales ignite,
We glimpse the magic cloaked in light.
To wonder is to feel alive,
In every heartbeat, dreams derive.

The Guideposts of the Heart

Maps drawn in ink of dreams untold,
Mark the paths where courage unfolds.
In shadows cast, we find our way,
With every choice, our spirits sway.

Embrace the signs that light the road,
In love's embrace, we'll bear our load.
The heart's own compass, trusted and true,
Leads us to places bold and new.

Skylarks and Silver Linings

When daylight breaks, the skylarks sing,
A joyous tune—life's offering.
Through every storm, a glimmer shines,
In darkest days, hope intertwines.

With silver linings draped in grace,
We find our strength, embrace the pace.
In laughter bright, our worries fade,
Together, brighter futures are made.

Treading the Traces of Tomorrow

In the quiet dawn, we tread our way,
Footprints whisper dreams of a brighter day.
Each step a choice, each breath a chance,
We weave our fates in a sacred dance.

The path ahead is veiled in mist,
With every turn, let hope persist.
Through shadows long and light anew,
The traces guide us to what is true.

Ascending the Peaks of Belief

Upon the slopes where courage climbs,
Each heartbeat echoes in timeless rhymes.
With hands outstretched, we reach for skies,
In every struggle, our spirit flies.

The summit glows with a golden light,
A beacon bright in the endless night.
With every breath, our hearts unite,
Ascending peaks, embracing the heights.

The Melody of Unseen Wings

In twilight's glow, a whisper stirs,
A song of wings that gently purrs.
Invisible threads weave through the air,
Creating symphonies beyond compare.

Each note a dream, each chord a sigh,
The melody dances where shadows lie.
Listen closely, let your spirit sway,
To the unseen wings that guide our way.

Lifting Hearts to Celestial Heights

Beneath the stars, we raise our hands,
In unity, the universe understands.
With each heartbeat, we ascend the night,
Lifting our souls, embracing the light.

Together we rise, a radiant force,
Charting the skies as we steer our course.
With faith as our compass, we'll ignite,
Lifting hearts to celestial heights.

Ascending Through the Clouds

A whisper rides the breeze above,
Soft wings of dreams unfurl with love.
Through the mist, the visions sway,
In a dance where night meets day.

Each step a leap into the light,
Hearts embrace the gentle flight.
Clouds cradle hopes, a vast expanse,
Where every soul can find its chance.

With colors bright and shadows bold,
New stories in the sky unfold.
Upward bound, we shed our fears,
In the heights, we find our years.

Together we will rise and soar,
To realms untouched, forevermore.
A journey made on faith and trust,
In the clouds, our hearts combust.

Lifting Hearts to Celestial Heights

Beneath the stars, we raise our hands,
In unity, the universe understands.
With each heartbeat, we ascend the night,
Lifting our souls, embracing the light.

Together we rise, a radiant force,
Charting the skies as we steer our course.
With faith as our compass, we'll ignite,
Lifting hearts to celestial heights.

Ascending Through the Clouds

A whisper rides the breeze above,
Soft wings of dreams unfurl with love.
Through the mist, the visions sway,
In a dance where night meets day.

Each step a leap into the light,
Hearts embrace the gentle flight.
Clouds cradle hopes, a vast expanse,
Where every soul can find its chance.

With colors bright and shadows bold,
New stories in the sky unfold.
Upward bound, we shed our fears,
In the heights, we find our years.

Together we will rise and soar,
To realms untouched, forevermore.
A journey made on faith and trust,
In the clouds, our hearts combust.

The Canvas of Possibility

Beneath the stars, a blank design,
The canvas calls, both yours and mine.
With every stroke, our dreams ignite,
Creating worlds in shades of light.

Daring thoughts begin to blend,
In colors bright, our spirits mend.
Brushes dipped in hope and grace,
We paint our path, our sacred space.

Each hue a chance, each line a claim,
In this vast realm, we stake our name.
Imagination, wild and free,
The masterpiece of you and me.

With every heart that dares to dream,
We weave the fabric of our theme.
In this gallery, we are the art,
Crafting futures, a brand new start.

Beyond the Limits of Gravity

In realms where physics bends and sways,
A dance of light in endless ways.
We challenge the chains that hold us near,
And venture forth without a fear.

Stars whisper secrets, ancient and wise,
Inviting us to claim the skies.
With every heartbeat, we rise anew,
Defying limits, breaking through.

No anchor binds the soul's intent,
In this vast void, our dreams are sent.
We float on breezes of pure design,
In the cosmos' arms, our spirits shine.

The ground below, a distant thought,
In orbits free, our battles fought.
Beyond the pull, we find our way,
To realms where night transforms to day.

A Symphony of Unseen Futures

In silence lies a melody,
A whispering sound, just wait and see.
The notes of dreams entwined with hope,
Creating paths where hearts can cope.

Each soul a string, a vibrant tune,
Together sung beneath the moon.
We harmonize with every tear,
An echo of that deep held fear.

In shadows cast by what's to come,
We find our place, where beats succumb.
The rhythm pulses, strong and true,
In this dance of life, a world anew.

With every note, a future spins,
A symphony where each heart wins.
Though unseen paths may twist and wind,
Together, we weave what's undefined.

Untamed Journeys Above

Wings unfurl in the azure sky,
Clouds whisper secrets as we fly.
Mountains beckon, vast and grand,
Instincts guide us, unplanned.

Rivers sparkle, dancing light,
Chasing dreams, hearts take flight.
Horizons call with siren's song,
In this space, we all belong.

Wild winds carry our souls free,
Boundless wonders, you and me.
Stars ignite the dusky night,
Together, we embrace the height.

Unchained spirit, brave and bold,
Every story waits to be told.
Through the storms, we brave the tide,
In untamed journeys, we take pride.

Daring to Touch the Stars

With every wish, we cast our dreams,
Reaching high, or so it seems.
Galaxies whisper, beckoning bright,
In the depth of the endless night.

Comets race, a fleeting glance,
In their trails, we find our chance.
Navigating through the dark,
In the silence, we leave our mark.

Celestial wonders guide our way,
In starlit paths, we choose to stay.
A dance of fire, a spark of hope,
Through cosmic seas, we learn to cope.

Together we light the endless night,
Daring hearts in the quiet flight.
For every star within our reach,
A universe of dreams we teach.

The Soaring Heart's Odyssey

Beyond the mountains, far and wide,
The heart leaps forth, the soul our guide.
From valleys low to peaks that gleam,
We chase the rhythm of the dream.

In the stillness, the whispers grow,
Every heartbeat, a tale to show.
Through trials faced with courage fair,
We rise above, entwined in air.

With open arms, we greet the dawn,
Lessons learned as shadows yawn.
Each challenge met, a token worn,
From every struggle, we are reborn.

So take the leap, embrace the flight,
For soaring hearts will find their light.
In odysseys, forever roam,
Together, we create our home.

Weaving Tapestries of Belief

In threads of hope, our tales are spun,
Colorful patterns, hearts beat as one.
Each knot a story, woven tight,
In the fabric of our shared light.

Dreams entwined in vibrant hue,
Uniting paths, the old and new.
In every stitch, a vision clear,
We weave a world, our voices near.

With gentle hands, we shape our fate,
Bridging divides that often create.
In unity, we find our strength,
Through woven bonds, we go the length.

So let us gather, rich and bold,
Creating tapestries finely told.
In the embrace of belief's sweet grace,
We find our place, our sacred space.

The Alchemy of Sweet Dreams

In twilight's glow, the shadows wane,
Whispers of hope call softly again.
Stars sprinkle wishes, gentle and bright,
As sleep unfolds its wings of night.

A canvas of dreams where wishes reside,
Each thread woven with love as its guide.
A dance of colors, a melody sweet,
In the heart's quiet realm, we find our retreat.

Embracing the Sky's Embrace

The horizon stretches, a canvas so vast,
Where earth meets the heavens, a spell is cast.
With arms open wide, we rise and we soar,
In the heart of the sky, we find our explore.

Clouds dance like whispers, light as a sigh,
Painting the blue of a limitless sky.
Each breath a reminder, each moment a gift,
In the caress of the winds, our spirits uplift.

Feathered Hopes in the Wind

Like feathers adrift on a gentle breeze,
Hopes take to flight, our worries appease.
Each flutter a promise, a vision in flight,
Chasing the dawn, embracing the light.

With faith as our compass, through storms we will glide,
Seeking horizons where dreams can reside.
In the heart of the tempest, we trust and we bend,
For every broken wing, a new chance to mend.

Rhapsody of the Airborne Heart

In the dance of the leaves, a rhapsody sings,
The pulse of the earth in the flight of the wings.
Songs of the sky, a serenade bold,
Stories of love and of dreams to unfold.

With laughter as sunlight, and tears as the rain,
We rise on the currents, free of all pain.
In every heartbeat, the worlds intertwine,
A tapestry woven in love's sweet design.

Soaring Beyond the Horizon

With wings of hope, we take the flight,
Chasing dreams that beckon bright.
The sun sets low, a golden hue,
We find our strength in skies so blue.

Through clouds of doubt, we rise and glide,
Exploring worlds that stretch wide.
Each heartbeat sings a daring song,
In the vast unknown, we belong.

The winds of change, they lift us high,
Painting visions across the sky.
With every breath, we push the pace,
In quest of freedom, we find our place.

Soaring forth, we leave the shore,
Embracing all that life has in store.
Together we venture, hand in hand,
Soaring beyond what we had planned.

Echoes of Aspirations

Whispers of dreams dance in the air,
Echoes of hopes, fragile yet fair.
In quiet moments, they softly call,
Reminding us to rise, never fall.

With every step, the echoes grow loud,
Amongst the silence, we stand proud.
Through trials faced and lessons learned,
Our aspirations for greatness burned.

In shadows cast by doubt and fear,
We push ahead, the vision is clear.
United in purpose, we sing our song,
In the realm of dreams, we all belong.

May these echoes guide our way,
Lighting paths where shadows play.
Together we soar, hearts aligned,
In the garden of hopes, love intertwined.

Wings of the Imagination

Imagination takes us where we dream,
On vibrant wings, we float and beam.
Each thought a feather, soft and light,
We journey far, into the night.

In colors bright and shades of bold,
We paint our stories, yet untold.
With every whisper, tales unfold,
In realms of wonder, we dare to hold.

The skies invite with open hands,
Letting minds soar to distant lands.
Adventure calls, we heed the sound,
In the depths of dreams, magic found.

With wings outstretched, we find our flight,
Navigating through the stars so bright.
Together we chase the endless skies,
On wings of thought, we shall arise.

The Journey of Stardust

Born from the night, we trace our roots,
A journey forged in cosmic pursuits.
Stardust glimmers in the vast unknown,
Guiding our hearts, where dreams are sown.

With every step on this celestial shore,
We gather light, forevermore.
In galaxies vast, we weave our tale,
A tapestry stitched where hopes set sail.

Through nebulae bright and comets' glow,
We seek the paths that stars bestow.
The journey unfolds, a wondrous flight,
In the dance of cosmos, hearts ignite.

As stardust whispers secrets divine,
We cherish the journey, yours and mine.
Together we soar, side by side,
In the universe's arms, we abide.

The Rise of Pastel Dreams

In twilight tones, the skies awake,
Soft hues dance, the shadows break.
Whispers call from fields afar,
As dreams ignite like evening stars.

A canvas brushed with gentle light,
Mornings glisten, banishing night.
With every stroke, the heart will sigh,
Painting hopes that never die.

Clouds like cotton, soft and free,
Cradle thoughts like memories.
Each breath holds a promise anew,
In pastel shades where love shines through.

Together we chase the daylight's gleam,
In the rise of our pastel dream.
Hand in hand, we shall explore,
The realms of colors, forevermore.

Souls Adrift in the Breeze

Whispers of longing through branches sway,
Souls adrift in the wind's soft play.
Carried forth on trails unseen,
Where echoes linger, pale and keen.

Gentle hearts woven in time,
Tales of joy, tales sublime.
Underneath the open sky,
Beneath the branches, dreams shall fly.

Caught in the currents, we softly spin,
With laughter's notes, we begin.
Embracing the world, so vast and wide,
In the breeze, we learn to glide.

Together we'll dance on the airs that rise,
Souls adrift where the spirit flies.
Through every moment, in every sough,
We find ourselves forever now.

A Serenade of Infinite Visions

A serenade hums beneath the stars,
Infinite visions in cosmic bars.
Melodies echo through the night,
Opening doors to realms of light.

Each note a pathway, each chord a chance,
Guiding us in the cosmic dance.
A tapestry woven of dreams and sighs,
Where aspirations touch the skies.

Through shadows deep, we wander free,
In the symphony of eternity.
With each heartbeat, a story unfolds,
In the warmth of the universe, we behold.

Together we dream of what lies ahead,
In this serenade, our hearts are fed.
Infinite visions, forever entwined,
In the music of life, our spirits aligned.

Sailing Through Realms Unknown

Set our sails to the winds of fate,
Sailing through realms we navigate.
With every wave, we find our way,
Charting courses where dreams will stay.

Stars our guide in the inky sea,
Whispers of destiny calling me.
With courage bold, we face the night,
In search of wonders, pure delight.

Across horizons, the dawn will break,
New adventures, the heart will take.
With each swell, we grow to know,
The beauty found in the ebb and flow.

Together we journey, side by side,
In this vast ocean, our hearts abide.
Sailing through dreams, a love that's shown,
In realms unknown, we claim our own.

The Symphony of the Airborne

In lofty heights where eagles soar,
The whispers of the winds implore.
Melodies of freedom, soaring high,
Echoing through the boundless sky.

Wings spread wide, embracing grace,
Nature's song in this sacred space.
Each note a tale, a story spun,
In the symphony where dreams begun.

Clouds drift softly, a gentle dance,
In every breeze, a fleeting chance.
Harmony of life takes flight,
A serenade in fading light.

Beneath the stars, the nightingale,
Sings of journeys where hearts prevail.
In the silence, a pure refrain,
The symphony of hope remains.

Embracing the Infinite Sky

Beneath the expanse, vast and blue,
Where dreams are born and hopes renew.
The canvas stretches, bold and wide,
Inviting souls to take a ride.

With every dawn, the sun ignites,
Painting the world with golden lights.
The clouds, like whispers, dance and sway,
In this embrace of endless day.

The horizon beckons, calling clear,
A promise of adventures near.
In stillness found among the heights,
We reach for stars, igniting nights.

Together we stand, hand in hand,
Touched by the magic of this land.
In the breeze, our spirits high,
We are but whispers in the sky.

The Journey Beyond the It's   to Be

Paths untraveled stretch ahead,
With every step, we weave our thread.
In shadows cast, the light breaks through,
A journey starts with a view anew.

The mountains loom, their peaks so grand,
With dreams in tow, we'll make our stand.
In valleys low, where shadows play,
We find our strength in night and day.

Each choice a compass, guiding us,
Through tempest's roar, in quiet trust.
The road may twist, and winds may bend,
But within our hearts, we know the end.

With every heartbeat, bold and free,
We navigate through what's meant to be.
In the endless quest, we forge our fate,
The journey calls, we cannot wait.

Ascending the Dreamer's Staircase

Steps of hope, in silence tread,
To heights where dreamers fear to tread.
Each rise a whisper, soft and pure,
In the ascent, we find our cure.

The staircase spirals, wide and grand,
An invitation to take a stand.
With every footfall, spirits soar,
Each level brings us closer to more.

In shadows dim, the light will gleam,
A guiding star, a cherished dream.
Embrace the climb, for all we seek,
Is found in strength when we feel weak.

Atop the heights, the world laid bare,
In breaths of wonder, we declare.
With hearts ablaze, we rise as one,
At the summit, our journey's won.

The Promises of an Open Sky

Beneath the vast, unbroken blue,
Dreams swirl like dandelions in the breeze.
Hope whispers softly, ever true,
As shadows fade, and the heart finds ease.

Birds sing loudly, their praises soar,
Each note a promise of freedom's delight.
The horizon beckons, forever more,
Embracing dusk, embracing light.

In the tapestry of twilight's glow,
Stars emerge, a sprinkle of fate.
With every breath, the wonders flow,
In an open sky where dreams await.

Thus we wander, hand in hand,
With whispered secrets carried on high.
Together we'll trace this limitless land,
Under the promises of an open sky.

Celestial Graffiti of the Mind

Thoughts collide like meteors bright,
Scribbling stories across the void.
Each flicker a spark, igniting the night,
In the cosmos of dreams, we're overjoyed.

Colors dance upon the canvas wide,
As constellations weave their magic here.
In this theater, we take great pride,
Each brushstroke a vision, crystal clear.

Beyond the stars, our spirits flow,
In abstract forms, we find our place.
Every moment echoes, every glow,
Marking the universe with our trace.

So let the wild visions unfurl,
Painting the skies, transcending time.
In the limitless realm of a dreaming world,
We etch our legacy, eternally sublime.

Questing Beyond the Clouds

With courage stowed in pockets deep,
We venture forth on pathways high.
Guided by dreams that never sleep,
Our hearts alight, as hope draws nigh.

Each step a dance on soft, white mist,
As wonders wait in the boundless blue.
With every sigh, a wish persists,
A whispered promise long overdue.

Beyond the clouds, the sun awaits,
Revealing stories lost to time.
Together we break through heaven's gates,
In this infinite realm that feels so prime.

Let us quest where the wild winds blow,
With open hearts and daring minds.
The journey calls, the spirits glow,
In realms unknown, our destiny finds.

Ethereal Explorations of the Spirit

In the stillness beneath the stars,
We travel realms where visions gleam.
Each moment an echo of who we are,
Floating softly on life's gentle stream.

Wings unfurled as the silence speaks,
With whispers that tickle the edges of thought.
In the depths of the heart, intuition peaks,
Secrets unfurling, forever sought.

Dance with the shadows and the light,
As time dissolves into endless waves.
In the heart's pulse, the infinite night,
Calls us to dream, to be brave.

So let us wander, explore the soul,
In the ethereal night, we take flight.
In every heartbeat, we feel the whole,
A journey of spirit, pure and bright.

Sketches of a Dreamer's Sky

In twilight's hue, the stars appear,
With whispered hopes that line the sphere.
Each flicker tells a tale of light,
A canvas vast, beyond the night.

Clouds drift softly, dreams take flight,
Their shadows dance in silver white.
From whispered thoughts, new worlds are spun,
In the dreamer's sky, all is begun.

The moon a guide on paths unclear,
Through cosmic trails, we persevere.
With every sigh, the night expands,
As visions bloom in gentle hands.

In this realm where visions meet,
The sketcher's heart finds joy complete.
Through every color, every sigh,
A masterpiece of dreams will lie.

An Odyssey of Broken Chains

Once forged in fire, they held us tight,
But whispered winds blew through the night.
With every clash, a promise made,
We break the bonds that held us, frayed.

The road ahead is wild and wide,
With courage found, we'll turn the tide.
Each step we take, a voice reclaimed,
In unity, we're not ashamed.

The weight of chains now lost in dust,
The spark of freedom is our trust.
Together we soar, a fearless band,
Forging paths across the land.

Through trials faced and battles fought,
Our spirits rise, our souls are caught.
With hearts ablaze, we chase the sun,
An odyssey that has begun.

Flight of the Unwritten

In pages blank, the silence hums,
A universe where nobody comes.
With ink untouched, the dreams ignite,
And soar beyond the edge of night.

Each thought a feather, light and free,
As whispers craft our destiny.
Through realms unseen, our spirits glide,
In every heart, the stories hide.

The quill may tremble, yet it knows,
With every stroke, a tale that flows.
A dance of words in shadows cast,
Unwritten journeys, hold them fast.

In twilight's glow, the stories bloom,
A vivid world released from gloom.
The flight begins, and hearts align,
In realms of dreams, our souls entwine.

A Tapestry of Wishes

Threads of hope in colors bright,
Woven gently, day and night.
Every wish a stitch, a tie,
In this fabric, dreams can fly.

Patterns of laughter, tears, and grace,
Life's rich tapestry we embrace.
Each moment stitched, a tale retold,
In warmth and shade, in bright and bold.

The loom of time hums soft and low,
Creating tales from all we sow.
With every heart, the pattern grows,
In this masterpiece, our spirit shows.

As wishes meld and colors blend,
In unity, we find our end.
A tapestry, both grand and dear,
In every thread, our wishes clear.

Celestial Echoes of Desire

In the night sky, whispers bloom,
Starry dreams cast away gloom.
Hearts align in cosmic dance,
Echoes of hope, a fleeting chance.

Fires ignite in silken air,
Fate weaves its threads with care.
Desires burn like distant suns,
Chasing shadows, love outruns.

Tides of passion rise and fall,
Moonlit secrets softly call.
In the stillness, spirits soar,
Celestial echoes forevermore.

Floating Through the Mirage

Waves of sand in twilight's glow,
Illusions dance, a soft tableau.
Dreams dissolving in the heat,
Footsteps vanish, love's retreat.

Colors blend, a vibrant show,
Mirage whispers, soft and low.
Holding tight to fleeting grace,
Time's embrace, a warm embrace.

Through the haze, the heart does roam,
In the mirage, we find home.
Floating gently, lost yet found,
In this world, we're tightly bound.

A Lantern Against the Night

In the darkness, a flicker bright,
A lantern glows, defying night.
Guiding paths through shadows deep,
A gentle promise, faith to keep.

In still moments, truth unfolds,
Warmth within, as fear beholds.
Light that dances, softly sways,
Chasing doubts and shadowed ways.

A beacon for the wandering heart,
In solitude, it plays a part.
With every flicker, courage grows,
In the night, our spirit glows.

The Guiding Light of Ambition

A spark ignites beneath the stars,
A vision born, dreams travel far.
Each step forward, a bold embrace,
Chasing goals, we find our place.

Through the struggle, we endure,
Ambition's fire, fierce and pure.
With every challenge, strength reveals,
A guiding light, passion heals.

In the depths of night, we rise,
Chasing dawn beyond the skies.
With hearts ablaze, we strive and fight,
For our dreams, the guiding light.

Elysium Awaits in the Clouds

Above the world, where dreams do drift,
A realm of light, a gentle gift.
In whispered winds, the secrets call,
Elysium awaits, beyond us all.

The skies embrace our deepest sighs,
Enfolded in hues where hope never dies.
A sanctuary, so pure, so bright,
Where shadows fade and souls take flight.

Drifting softly on cotton wings,
In silence, tune to what joy brings.
Each heartbeat syncs with the cosmic play,
Elysium beckons, come what may.

So close your eyes, let your spirit rise,
In clouds of peace, where wonder lies.
A journey awaits, so vast and free,
Elysium calls, for you and me.

Unchained Aspirations in Flight

A flicker of hope, a spark ignite,
With wings unfurled, we chase the light.
Beyond the chains that once held tight,
Unchained aspirations soar in flight.

We carve the sky with dreams untold,
Embrace the warmth, let courage unfold.
With every heartbeat, a chance we find,
To leave the past and redefine.

The winds of change, they whisper clear,
In every note, we find our cheer.
With eyes set high, we break the mold,
Our story's written in threads of gold.

As horizons blend with sunsets bold,
Together we rise, no fears to hold.
In this expanse where hearts unite,
We dance through dreams, unchained in flight.

Wings of the Whimsical

In the quiet whispers of the night,
Magic glimmers, soft and slight.
With wings of grace, in colors bright,
The whimsical dance takes its flight.

Each flutter tells of tales anew,
As stars above glance down in view.
With laughter woven in the breeze,
We float like feathers, at ease.

Through cotton candy skies we soar,
With every turn, we seek for more.
Imagination spins a web of dreams,
In the whimsical world, nothing's as it seems.

So let your spirit wander free,
Embrace the wonder, let it be.
On wings of whimsy, take your part,
In every flight, live with your heart.

A Horizon Beyond the Ordinary

In the dawn's embrace, we stand aligned,
With visions clear, and hopes refined.
A horizon beckons, vast and wide,
Beyond the ordinary, where dreams reside.

Each step we take, through fields of gold,
Unfolding stories yet to be told.
With spirits bold, we venture forth,
To seek the treasures of our worth.

The sky ignites in fiery hues,
Awakening the wonders we choose.
Together we chase the setting sun,
In this journey, we are never done.

So rise with the tides, let your heart sing,
For within every moment lies the spring.
A horizon awaits, just out of sight,
Beyond the ordinary, into the light.

Floating on Gossamer Clouds

High above the world we soar,
In dreams where spirits freely explore.
Whispers of the breeze delight,
Carrying us through day and night.

Softly gliding, hearts entwined,
In a realm where stars align.
Gossamer threads of light embrace,
Guiding us in this sacred space.

Drifting gently, fears released,
Amongst the heavens, life's sweet feast.
With each breath, we dare to sing,
Floating high, our souls take wing.

Together on this journey bold,
Where every moment must be told.
In timeless air, we find our way,
Floating high, we greet the day.

The Dance of Possibility

In a world where dreams collide,
Life unfolds in rhythms tied.
Every step a choice to make,
Together we embrace the break.

With a twirl beneath the stars,
We rewrite fate, erase the scars.
Hands in hands, we leap afar,
Chasing hopes, we find our spark.

Through the shadows, visions glow,
In this dance, our spirits flow.
With each heartbeat, paths reveal,
A tapestry of boundless zeal.

Listen close, the music plays,
Guiding us through endless days.
In each twinkle, futures bright,
The dance of possibility ignites.

A Symphony of Aspirations

Notes of hope in the softest air,
A symphony beyond compare.
Strings of dreams in harmony,
Chords of passion, wild and free.

Winds of change whisper the tune,
Under the guidance of the moon.
Every note tells tales of old,
In this melody, dreams unfold.

Echoes of a fierce desire,
Burning like an endless fire.
Together we compose our song,
In unity, we all belong.

With each crescendo, hearts align,
Creating magic, hearts combine.
A symphony of hopes embraced,
In dreams, our spirits are placed.

Echoes of a Bright Tomorrow

In the silence, futures call,
Echoes whisper, rise and fall.
Sunlight dances on the face,
Promising hope, a warm embrace.

Steps we take, a path to share,
In every heartbeat, dreams laid bare.
Together weaving threads of light,
Echoes guiding through the night.

With each dawning of the sun,
New beginnings, we've just begun.
In every shadow, strength we find,
Echoes of a life defined.

Hope resounds, a melody,
Speaking truths for all to see.
In tomorrow's arms, we trust,
Echoes of dreams, in us, a must.

Horizons of Longing and Light

Beyond the hills, the sunlight gleams,
Whispers of hope paint the streams.
Each ray holds secrets, dreams untold,
Upon the canvas, stories unfold.

In the twilight, shadows play,
Yearning hearts drift away.
Every color, a tale of grace,
Longing finds its sacred space.

The horizon beckons with sweet embrace,
Revealing paths through time and space.
Where desires meet the open sky,
Bright futures call, as moments fly.

With every dawn, we rise again,
Collecting love, dispersing pain.
Horizons stretch, forever bright,
In the dance of longing and light.

A Mosaic of Inspired Flight

Beneath the clouds, the dreams align,
Fleeting whispers, a sacred sign.
Each moment captured, colors bright,
A mosaic formed in inspired flight.

Wings unfurl as dawn's embrace,
Guiding hearts through vast, open space.
Every heartbeat, a rhythm true,
In the dance of skies, we find anew.

Fragments of laughter, stories shared,
As the wind carries, we are bared.
In unity, our spirits soar,
A tapestry woven forevermore.

From dusk to dawn, our journey flows,
In the winds of change, our essence grows.
A mosaic bright, we take our flight,
Chasing the stars in the velvet night.

Cradled by the Air

In gentle breezes, soft and fair,
We find our peace, cradled by air.
Floating dreams, both near and far,
Guided lightly by a morning star.

Whispers of freedom fill the skies,
As laughter weaves through hollow sighs.
Each sigh a promise, held so close,
In the heart's cocoon, where love will grow.

Suspended in moments, time stands still,
Embracing dreams that dare to spill.
With every breath, the world awakens,
Cradled in air, our souls unshaken.

Together we rise, hand in hand,
Chasing the light, where shadows stand.
Through currents warm, our spirits flare,
For in this life, we're cradled by air.

Unwritten Chapters of the Sky

In the expanse, our stories blend,
Unwritten pages, on dreams we depend.
Stars are the ink, and clouds the sheet,
Every heartbeat a tale, bittersweet.

Horizons whisper the paths we chase,
Where destinies linger, waiting their place.
Each sunset paints a fresh new start,
Unwritten chapters that stir the heart.

As the moonlight spills on midnight streams,
We craft our futures from fragile dreams.
In the silence, a promise, we find,
A testament written in the night sky, blind.

Together we soar on wings of fate,
In the boundless sky, we contemplate.
With every dawn, we sketch our lives,
In unwritten chapters, our spirit thrives.

Journey of the Fearless Spirit

Through valleys deep and mountains high,
The spirit roams, it dares to fly.
With every step, it learns and grows,
Embracing fears that life bestows.

In shadows cast by doubt and pain,
Resilient hearts will break the chain.
They rise like suns at dawn's first light,
Igniting paths that feel so right.

Across the seas in storms that rage,
The fearless spirit turns the page.
With courage firm, they sail the tides,
Finding strength where hope abides.

Together we will face the fight,
United souls, our hearts ignited.
In journeys new, let spirits soar,
With fearless hearts, forevermore.

The Canvas of Endless Possibilities

With brush in hand, we start to dream,
A canvas wide, a vibrant stream.
Colors blend in limitless ways,
Creating visions that amaze.

Each stroke a whisper, bold and bright,
Revealing paths of pure delight.
Imagination drapes the scene,
In hues of joy and shades of green.

No boundaries hold the heart in place,
For every dream, there's wide embrace.
We paint our lives with endless grace,
In every line, we find our space.

Together we explore the light,
Transforming darkness into bright.
The canvas sings, our spirits free,
In endless possibilities.

Skylines of the Imagination

Above the clouds, where dreams reside,
The skylines form with heart as guide.
Each tower built of hopes and schemes,
A testament to vibrant dreams.

With every thought, new heights we gain,
In realms where wonders break the chain.
We glimpse the stars, so bright, so near,
In visions vast, we banish fear.

The structures rise where spirits soar,
Infinite dreams forevermore.
In cities crafted from our mind,
The beauty of the lost we find.

Through open skies our hearts will sail,
With courage strong, we shall not fail.
In skylines bright, our dreams align,
In endless flight, our spirits shine.

Chronicles of the Skylark

In fields of gold, the skylark sings,
Her melodies, like gentle wings.
A story told in tunes so sweet,
Of love and life, of loss and feats.

From dawn till dusk, her voice takes flight,
A symphony of pure delight.
Each note a whisper to the skies,
A tale of hope that never dies.

She dances through the morning mist,
While sunbeams warm her joyful tryst.
In every chord, a heart laid bare,
A testament of strength and care.

Chronicles of the sky she weaves,
Where dreams are born, and spirit believes.
With every song, she breaks the dark,
A guiding light, the brave skylark.

Whispers of Tomorrow

In the quiet glow of dawn,
Dreams begin to dance and sway.
Hope emerges softly drawn,
Painting visions of the day.

Echoes of a future bright,
Breathe the air, embrace the light.
Every whisper, every call,
Leads us onward through it all.

Time spins threads of silent gold,
Tales of courage yet untold.
With each heartbeat, we pursue,
Whispers leading me to you.

In the stillness of the night,
Stars align with a gentle might.
Tomorrow's promise waits in line,
A tender touch, a heart's design.

Flight Paths of the Heart

Two souls sail on winds of grace,
Through the clouds, they find their place.
With every glance, with every sigh,
They paint the vast, uncaring sky.

Fear dissolves in a tender flight,
Hearts entwined in the soft twilight.
Every twist, each swirling turn,
Brings them closer, hearts that burn.

Across horizons, bright and wide,
Together, they will always glide.
On currents of dreams, they will soar,
In the silence, they want more.

With wings spread out, they learn to trust,
To navigate through storms and dust.
In the journey, love will chart,
The endless flight paths of the heart.

Chasing Celestial Visions

Underneath a moonlit sky,
Wishes flutter, hopes will fly.
Stars like diamonds drip and fall,
Painting dreams, they heed the call.

Through the veil of midnight blue,
Chasing visions, brave and true.
Every glimmer tells a tale,
In the silence, hearts prevail.

Across the cosmos, they will chase,
Patterns form in endless space.
With each heartbeat, new designs,
Chasing visions, love aligns.

Bound by light, they dance and weave,
In the dreams, they dare believe.
Celestial whispers guide their course,
Chasing visions, pure of force.

Skylines of Desire

In the twilight, colors blend,
Shadowed lines stretch without end.
City lights like stars begin,
Whispering tales of where we've been.

Hearts align with the setting sun,
Chasing dreams, we've just begun.
In the spaces between the streets,
Desire flourishes and beats.

Underneath the vast expanse,
Fates entwined in this sweet chance.
With every heartbeat, sparks ignite,
Skylines such a wondrous sight.

In the glow of urban grace,
We discover our own place.
With every step, the world is ours,
Skylines filled with shining stars.

The Alchemy of Aspirations

In dreams, we weave our golden threads,
Whispers of hope, where ambition spreads.
Each spark ignites the fire within,
Transforming wishes, where journeys begin.

With potions brewed from heart's desire,
We mix our courage, fuel the fire.
In every heartbeat, a story unfolds,
The art of becoming, the brave and the bold.

Through trials faced and mountains climbed,
In each failure, a lesson chimed.
Alchemy turns the lead into gold,
A symphony of dreams, waiting to be told.

So let us dance in the moon's sweet light,
With every breath, we take our flight.
The alchemy of hopes, forever in sight,
Guiding our souls through the vast night.

Beyond the Edge of Sleep

Where shadows whisper and visions play,
Beyond the edge, night turns to day.
In dreams we travel, lost in the mist,
Awakening wonders, still unkissed.

Time stands still in that sacred space,
Where thoughts entwine in soft embrace.
The veil between, so thin and light,
Guides us gently to morning bright.

Drifting softly on silent wings,
The heart knows secrets that twilight sings.
In that darkness, a truth comes alive,
Nurturing hopes that silently strive.

So roam we must, where night meets dawn,
In every slumber, a world reborn.
Beyond the edge, find what we seek,
In dreams we gather, the strong and the weak.

Boundless Ascent

The mountain looms, a giant's grace,
Each step we take, a sacred space.
With every breath, our spirits soar,
Boundless ascent, forevermore.

Through valleys deep and rivers wide,
Our hearts aligned, we brave the tide.
With each sunrise, a new chance gleams,
Igniting hope, fulfilling dreams.

The clouds, our friends, we greet with cheer,
Embracing heights, dismissing fear.
In unity, our strength combines,
A journey written in starry lines.

So climb with me, where eagles dare,
On paths unknown, our souls laid bare.
In boundless ascent, we find our song,
Together, where we truly belong.

The Evolution of Light

From cosmic birth, a spark ignites,
In every shadow, brilliance fights.
Through endless years, in cycles bound,
The evolution of light resounds.

In the dawn's embrace, we come alive,
Colors converge, and dreams contrive.
A symphony of radiance shines,
Illuminating paths, weaving designs.

With every heartbeat, a pulse of flame,
Transforming darkness, we rise, we claim.
Witness the change in every hue,
A testament to all that is true.

So let us shine, both near and far,
Guided by our own guiding star.
In the evolution of light, we trust,
Embracing all, in love we must.

Journey to the Realm of Possibility

A path unfolds beneath my feet,
Where dreams and shadows softly meet.
With every step, a whisper calls,
To venture where the wild heart sprawls.

The stars above begin to gleam,
As courage stirs the quiet dream.
I tread upon the bated breath,
For only here, I conquer death.

With open eyes, I greet the dawn,
Embracing worlds that I have drawn.
Each heartbeat sings a melody,
A symphony of possibility.

Into the realms where wonders play,
I chase the colors of the day.
For here, the limits fade away,
And hope ignites the brightest ray.

Embracing the Winds of Change

The winds arise, a gentle stir,
They whisper secrets, soft and pure.
I feel their breath upon my skin,
It's time to shed what lies within.

This road ahead, a twisting line,
Where every curve is yours, is mine.
I lift my hands to greet the breeze,
And let it carry me with ease.

The past, a shadow in my wake,
I welcome new paths I will take.
With every gust, I set my sail,
To chase the winds, I will not fail.

So here I stand, with heart ablaze,
Embracing change in myriad ways.
The journey calls, let's make a start,
For every wind ignites the heart.

Soaring Beyond the Horizon

I spread my wings, the sky my stage,
To dance with clouds, to turn the page.
With every flap, I leave the ground,
The horizon whispers, life unbound.

The sun ignites the dawn anew,
With colors vibrant, bold, and true.
Beyond the line where sky meets sea,
I find the dreams that set me free.

The whispers of the world below,
Encourage me to rise and glow.
For every challenge, I embrace,
I soar on high, I find my place.

With every heartbeat, skies extend,
Limitless where journeys blend.
Soaring far beyond the line,
I find my wings, my dreams align.

Wings of Imagination

In twilight's grace, my thoughts take flight,
With wings of dreams, I soar the night.
Each spark of hope ignites the air,
As visions dance without a care.

Upon the canvas of the stars,
I paint my dreams, I heal my scars.
With colors bright and strokes so free,
My wings of thought become my key.

I drift through realms of endless lore,
Where whispers of the heart explore.
Each fantasy, a tapestry,
Woven with threads of mystery.

So let me fly, for I am bold,
In worlds of wonder, tales unfold.
On wings of imagination bright,
I find my voice, I claim my light.

Horizons Painted in Gold

The sun dips low in the sky,
Brushing the clouds with a hue.
A canvas stretched wide and bold,
Whispers of dreams coming true.

Golden rays dance on the sea,
Reflecting on waves like a song.
Nature's palette set so free,
In this moment, we all belong.

Mountains cast shadows so vast,
Guardians of secrets untold.
With each sunrise, shadows pass,
Horizons painted in gold.

In twilight's embrace, we stand,
Holding the warmth of the light.
Together we trace through the land,
Chasing the day into night.

The Flight of Inner Wishes

Deep in the heart, wishes soar,
Like whispers riding the breeze.
They gather strength, wanting more,
Floating on hopes that never freeze.

With wings made from dreams unspun,
They flutter, they swoop, they glide.
Chasing the setting sun,
In the vast open sky, we confide.

Each wish a star shining bright,
Guiding our paths through the dark.
In the quiet embrace of night,
We find the courage to embark.

So let them take off and fly,
Across the horizon so wide.
In each heart, they can't deny,
The magic of dreams inside.

Sketching the Dreamscape

With a brush dipped in twilight,
I paint the realms of my mind.
Each stroke a soft lullaby,
Glimpses of worlds intertwined.

Mountains rise and rivers flow,
In a dance of colors so free.
Let imagination's winds blow,
Carrying dreams across the sea.

Clouds whisper tales from afar,
In the silence, listen and learn.
Every twinkle, every star,
Lights the way for the dreams that burn.

Sketching the lines of the night,
Where fantasy meets the real.
With every heartbeat, take flight,
In this dreamscape, I heal.

Glistening Paths of Enchantment

Beneath the moon's silver glow,
Paths glisten with luminous light.
Whispers of magic linger slow,
Guiding the lost through the night.

Each step brings a story to tell,
Beneath the ancient oak trees.
Nature spins her wondrous spell,
Drawing the wanderers with ease.

Stars above twinkle like gems,
In the quiet, hearts softly beat.
Following luminous hem,
Through the forest, where spirits meet.

In this realm where dreams arise,
Awake to the wonders each day.
Glistening paths under vast skies,
Lead us gently on our way.

Uplifted by Stardust

In the night sky, wonders gleam,
Whispers of dreams, soft as a stream.
Stars twinkle bright, guiding our way,
Uplifts our spirits, come what may.

With each glimmer, hope is reborn,
Dancing in light, from dusk till dawn.
Stardust falls, a gentle embrace,
Lifting our hearts to a sacred space.

We breathe in magic, we let it flow,
With every heartbeat, our true selves glow.
Luminous paths stretch far and wide,
In starlit realms, we find our guide.

Together we rise and brightly shine,
Uplifted by stardust, yours and mine.
In this celestial dance, we belong,
Forever entwined, in love's sweet song.

The Ethereal Garden of Aspirations

In a garden where wishes bloom,
Hope takes root, dispelling gloom.
Petals of dreams, in colors bright,
Nurtured by faith, and endless light.

Each seedling whispers, brave and true,
Tales of paths we dare pursue.
With gentle hands, we tend and care,
In this sacred space, our spirits share.

The breeze carries laughter, soft and free,
A melody woven in harmony.
In the embrace of this vibrant land,
Together we rise, hand in hand.

As stars above twinkle and gleam,
We cultivate our deepest dream.
In the ethereal garden, aspirations thrive,
In love and hope, we come alive.

Sailing on Silken Breaths

On the waves of whispers, we set sail,
Carried by moments, soft as a veil.
Silken breaths guide us to distant shores,
Where dreams awaken and spirit soars.

With hearts unburdened, we rise anew,
Adrift in the currents of skies so blue.
Our laughter dances on the gentle breeze,
In the canvas of life, we paint with ease.

Every heartbeat echoes in the night,
Floating on visions, everything feels right.
Together, we journey through twilight's grace,
Sailing on silken breaths, we embrace.

As the sun dips low, casting golden hues,
We chase our destinies, guided by Muse.
With each wave, we find our way back home,
On silken breaths, in oceans we roam.

Reflections of a Dawn Yet Unseen

In the hush of night, dreams take flight,
Whispers of dawn, a shimmering light.
Echoes of hope in shadows cast,
Reflections linger from futures past.

A tapestry woven with threads of gold,
Stories of courage, waiting to unfold.
In the silence, we ponder and yearn,
For the dawn's embrace, our spirits burn.

With every heartbeat, the world stands still,
A promise of morning, a radiant thrill.
Unveiling treasures in moments unseen,
Reflections shimmer, a pathway serene.

As anticipation swells with the night,
We trust in tomorrow, embrace the light.
In the reflections, our souls are keen,
Awakening dreams, of a dawn yet unseen.

The Whispering Winds of Tomorrow

The winds whisper tales untold,
Of dreams that shimmer like pure gold.
They carry hopes on gentle sighs,
Beneath the vast and endless skies.

Through fields of green, the echoes play,
Marking the dawn of a bright new day.
With every rustle, secrets unfold,
In the soft embrace of the brave and bold.

Together we dance with fleeting time,
In harmony, our spirits climb.
Embracing change as it comes near,
With every whisper, we conquer fear.

As shadows fade, our hearts align,
In the journey, the stars will shine.
The winds guide us where dreams take flight,
Revealing paths bathed in twilight.

Boundless Visions Above

In realms where dreams begin to soar,
Visions flicker, calling for more.
The canvas stretches wide and free,
Painting futures yet to be.

We reach for stars, both near and far,
Every wish a guiding star.
With open hearts, we learn to see,
The beauty found in what can be.

Among the clouds, our spirits rise,
Where imagination never dies.
Each thought a spark, igniting light,
Turning darkness into bright.

With every step, we pave the way,
Creating magic in the fray.
Boundless visions, forever flow,
In the wonders of tomorrow's glow.

Ascent of the Soul

Through valleys deep, where shadows loom,
We search for light that conquers gloom.
The journey of the soul unfolds,
In whispers soft, the truth beholds.

With trials faced and lessons learned,
A fire within us brightly burned.
Each step we take, the higher we climb,
Embracing love, transcending time.

Mountains high, we shall embrace,
In every challenge, find our place.
As echoes of the past collide,
We rise anew, with hearts open wide.

The ascent continues, a sacred rite,
Guided by love, we stand and fight.
No summit too steep, no valley too deep,
For the ascent of the soul, we keep.

Illuminated Skies of Hope

At dawn's first light, the skies ignite,
Colors bloom, chasing the night.
In every hue, a promise lies,
A world reborn beneath bright skies.

Hope dances lightly on the breeze,
Whispers of love through rustling leaves.
With open arms, we reach for more,
Embracing dreams we can't ignore.

Through storms that pass and clouds that roam,
We find our strength, we build a home.
In illuminated skies, we trust,
In the power of hope, we must.

Together we rise, hand in hand,
Creating futures, bold and grand.
With every heartbeat, the journey flows,
In illuminated skies, our spirit glows.

Reaching for the Untouched

In whispers soft, the dreams arise,
A tethered heart, beneath the skies.
With outstretched hands, we seek the light,
To touch the stars, to take our flight.

Among the shadows, secrets hide,
In every step, the world's a guide.
We yearn to grasp what's pure and true,
A canvas bright, in shades of blue.

The winds will carry our silent hymns,
As we explore the world's own whims.
Each moment brief, yet oh so vast,
A treasure trove, our shadows cast.

To reach beyond, to feel the thrill,
In untouched grace, we find the will.
With every breath, we start anew,
A journey vast, in skies of blue.

The Art of Rising

From winter's cold, we learn to grow,
In darkest nights, let courage show.
A phoenix born from ashes' grace,
We find our heart in every space.

The struggle weaves a tapestry,
Of hope and dreams, what's yet to be.
With every fall, we learn the song,
In harmony, we will belong.

A dance of life, with leaps of faith,
In every trial, we find our wraith.
Through storms we rise, like waves of grace,
The art of rising, a warm embrace.

With open wings, the skies we claim,
In unity, we fan the flame.
Each heartbeat strong, we shall endure,
For in our souls, we are the cure.

A Flutter of Ephemeral Wings

Butterflies drift on summer air,
With colors bright, they float with flair.
In fleeting dance, they share their song,
A moment's love that feels so strong.

Through petals soft, they find their way,
A gentle brush, in soft ballet.
From bloom to bloom, a tale is spun,
In whispered dreams, the day is won.

With fragile grace, they teach the heart,
That life's a canvas, a work of art.
Embrace the now, let go the past,
For fleeting joy holds moments vast.

In twilight hush, they bid farewell,
Their fleeting dance, a magic spell.
With every flutter, memories cling,
We cherish the touch of ephemeral wings.

Dawn of the Infinite

As morning breaks, the light does spill,
Awakening dreams, a quiet thrill.
In colors warm, the world ignites,
The dawn whispers with soft delights.

Horizons wide, our spirits soar,
In each new dawn, we seek for more.
The infinite paths, they call our name,
In every heartbeat, sparks the flame.

With every step, we weave the day,
In currents vast, we find our way.
The sun will rise, the shadows fade,
In light we trust, our fears betrayed.

The dawn of dreams, where hope resides,
In endless skies, our faith abides.
Together we chase the morning's kiss,
In every dawn, we find our bliss.

The Colors of Ambition

In the dawn of dreams, the colors rise,
Vivid strokes of hope paint the skies.
Each hue a whisper of goals untold,
Fires of desire in hearts so bold.

With every step, a vibrant trace,
The palette shifts in the fervent race.
Scarlet passion and azure grace,
Each one a part of this grand embrace.

Golden glimmers of futures bright,
Emerald visions take flight at night.
As shadows fade, colors intertwine,
In the canvas of life, forever shine.

Ambition's song in a chorus of cheers,
A tapestry woven from hopes and fears.
Together we thrive, through darkness and light,
With colors of ambition, we soar to new height.

Journey to the Stars

Beyond the blue where the dreams collide,
A journey begins where the brave reside.
With starlit paths, we chart our course,
Through galaxies vast, fueled by pure force.

Each twinkle a guide in the night so deep,
Whispers of wonders while we softly sleep.
In cosmic seas, we set our sail,
On celestial waves where hearts prevail.

Nebulae bloom in colors untold,
Stories of stardust, adventures unfold.
From planets unknown, we gather our light,
On this quest for the stars, daring and bright.

With each new dawn, we reach for the sky,
In the arms of the universe, forever we fly.
Journey to stars, where dreams intertwine,
In the fabric of cosmos, our souls align.

Chasing the Morning Light

With every dawn, the shadows retreat,
Golden rays dance on soft, cool streets.
Awakening hope with each bright glance,
Chasing the morning, we begin to chance.

Whispers of dawn call through the mist,
The world comes alive with a gentle twist.
Every flower opens, reaching for grace,
In the warmth of the sun, we find our place.

Joyful laughter fills the crisp air,
In the brilliance of day, troubles lay bare.
Chasing the morning, we seize the day,
With light as our guide, we'll find our way.

As night bids farewell and dreams take flight,
Grateful we stand, embraced by the light.
Together we rise, in joy and delight,
Chasing the morning, hearts ever bright.

Labyrinths of the Dreamer's Heart

In the labyrinth deep where shadows play,
Dreamers wander lost, seeking the way.
Each turn a secret, a story unfolds,
In the chambers of hope, where magic molds.

Whispers of wishes drift through the night,
Guiding the seekers toward radiant light.
With every heartbeat, a path is revealed,
Through the maze of the heart, truth is unsealed.

Mirrors reflect the fears that confound,
Yet courage emerges in silence profound.
Navigating winding, forgotten ways,
Beyond the dark corners, bright destiny stays.

For in the heart's core, the dreamers reside,
Finding their way with the stars as their guide.
In labyrinths woven with love and art,
They'll forge their own paths, the song of the heart.

Navigating the Stars

Beneath the midnight sky so vast,
We chart our dreams, connections cast.
With every twinkling point of light,
We find our way, embracing night.

The constellations guide our flight,
Through cosmic rivers, paths ignite.
In silence, whispers of the bold,
Their secrets long forgotten, told.

An astral map we seek to hold,
With stories woven, threads of gold.
We sail on hope, each star a flame,
Forever bound to the night's acclaim.

As dawn approaches, stars fade away,
Yet in our hearts, their glow will stay.
In endless skies, we'll travel far,
Forever dreams of navigating stars.

Horizons Painted in Hope

At dawn, a canvas bright and bold,
With strokes of pink and threads of gold.
Each sunrise whispers of new days,
A promise held in vibrant rays.

Mountains rise, kissing the sky,
With valleys deep, where dreams can lie.
In every shadow, tales unfold,
Horizons painted, dreams retold.

The winds of change will softly blow,
Through fields of dreams, a gentle flow.
With every step, we'll forge our path,
Chasing the light, escaping wrath.

So plant your seeds where hope can bloom,
And let love's fragrance fill the room.
For every dawn brings new delight,
Horizons painted, hearts take flight.

Soaring Over Boundless Skies

An eagle glides on thermals high,
Beneath the arch of endless sky.
With wings outstretched, we leave the ground,
In whispers soft, our hearts are found.

Above the clouds, where dreams reside,
We chase the sun, in winds we glide.
Through currents wild, we rise with grace,
Embracing freedom in this space.

The world below, a tapestry,
Of moments lived in memory.
As we ascend, our spirits soar,
Defying limits, yearning for more.

So join the flight, let worries cease,
And find your strength in boundless peace.
In every heartbeat, echoes cry,
Soaring high above the sky.

The Dance of Unfolding Realities

In twilight's glow, the shadows play,
As whispers shape the dawning day.
With every step, the world anew,
In swirling thoughts, our lives accrue.

The dance of fate, a gentle spin,
Revealing truths that lie within.
In every laugh, in every tear,
Unfolding paths that draw us near.

The universe winks, a secret shared,
In moments fleeting, hearts laid bare.
Together lost, yet found in dreams,
Where everything is not as it seems.

We weave the fabric of our days,
In colors bright, in subtle grays.
In harmony, our lives align,
The dance of reality, divine.

Milton Keynes UK
Ingram Content Group UK Ltd.
UKHW021928011224
451790UK00005B/71